How to Stay
Positive
in a Negative World

Andrew Wommack

© Copyright 2024 – Andrew Wommack

Printed in the United States of America. All rights reserved. No portion of this book may be reproduced, stored in a retrieval system, or transmitted in any form or by any means—electronic, mechanical, photocopy, recording, scanning, or other—except for brief quotations in critical reviews or articles, without the prior written permission of the publisher.

Unless otherwise indicated, all Scripture quotations are taken from the King James Version® of the Bible. Copyright © by the British Crown. Public domain.

All emphasis within Scripture quotations is the author's own.

Published in partnership between Andrew Wommack Ministries and Harrison House Publishers.

Woodland Park, CO 80863 – Shippensburg, PA 17257

ISBN 13 TP: 978-1-59548-666-0

For Worldwide Distribution, Printed in the USA

1 2 3 4 5 6 / 27 26 25 24

Contents

Introduction 1
Keep Your Eyes on God 3
Hope Deferred Makes the Heart Sick 5
Don't Let Your Heart Be Troubled 7
Do What Is Right 9
Don't Be Corrupted 11
Words Have Power 13
Get in the Word 16
Encourage Yourself in the Lord 18
Seek God's Wisdom 20
Renew Your Mind 22
Let Your Heart Rejoice 24
Keep Your Heart Clean 26
Don't Believe a Negative Report 27
You Don't Need All the Details 30
Personalize God's Promises............................. 32
Use Your Imagination 36
What Picture Is Inside You? 38
Don't Let Yourself Be Tempted 40
Draw on Your Relationship with God 42
Choose Your Mold... 44
Conclusion 46
Receive Jesus as Your Savior 51
Receive the Holy Spirit 53

Introduction

Do you find yourself discouraged because what you're believing for hasn't come to pass yet? Are you standing on God's promises, but you hear people contradict those promises with negativity and doubt? Do you follow the news of the world and wonder if it's only going to get worse?

There have been many times I've needed to stay positive when things didn't appear to be going our way.

Several years ago, we completed the first building on the campus of our Charis Bible College in Woodland Park, Colorado. It's what we now call The Barn. Some people just looked at all the negatives surrounding the project, but I just kept praising God! We went back and forth with the city to get building permits for some time after we purchased the property in 2009. We finally moved in on January 6, 2014, and we haven't looked back since!

Despite those challenges, I was able to rejoice because I didn't let myself get discouraged during that whole time. Now, I will admit, there was a time when I felt a righteous anger because we were facing some resistance, but I still didn't get discouraged. I just rebuked the devil, and we kept moving forward with our plans.

After that, we started making plans for our 3,200-seat auditorium. A person who worked for us at the time said, "Well, they got The Barn done, but there's no way they'll get The Auditorium done!" That person just had a negative outlook. They let circumstances dictate how they saw things rather than the Word of God.

You see, when we started, we just didn't have the resources to buy the land in Woodland Park. But with God, nothing is impossible! At the time of this writing, we have buildings and property worth more than $135 million, debt free. Praise the Lord!

God has put the vision for even more buildings in my heart, and by the time we are finished with our current plans, it may cost upward of $1 billion to build out our Charis campus with student housing, a recreation center, classroom space, and other things. That may sound daunting to some people, but I've learned to be encouraged and stay positive, even when my critics are being negative.

God is no respecter of persons. If the Lord can do it for me, I believe He can do it for you too. You've got to encourage yourself and stay positive in a negative world.

Keep Your Eyes on God

I will set no wicked thing before mine eyes: I hate the work of them that turn aside; it *shall not cleave to me.*

Psalm 101:3

I was raised in a Christian home in Texas. I was born again when I was eight years old, and my dad was one of the deacons in our church. As a child, I was just taught to love God. I probably heard about bad things in the world, but they didn't affect me, so I never thought about them. That kind of life just didn't even register with me.

Not long after I got really turned on to the Lord on March 23, 1968, my mother took me on a trip to Bern, Switzerland, for a Baptist youth conference with Billy Graham. Along the way, we stopped in New York City. We were staying in a hotel in Times Square, and I had never seen anything like what was going on around me—my jaw just dropped! But I had hundreds of Gospel tracts (small booklets), and I was excited about handing them out and witnessing for the Lord.

At about 2 a.m., I was walking down the alleys in the city. When I saw a group of people, I'd go up to them, pass out tracts, and tell them about the Lord. That may not have been smart, but because I was following God and not filling myself with the sewage of the world, I didn't even know enough to be afraid. I had zero fear. I shared the Gospel with these people who were probably up to no good, and I just cleared out all the alleys in the wee hours of the morning.

You might be reading this, thinking, *What's wrong with this guy?* Well, I eventually found out what kind of situation I had put myself in. (We'll finish this story later on!) But at the time, I was just loving God and living to serve Him and share Him with anyone no matter where I went. And in all the years since the Lord touched my life, I've stayed full of His love, and my relationship with Him is greater now than it's ever been.

Most Christians would never have the kind of experience I had in Times Square because they fill themselves with all the trash of this world. As a matter of fact, many of them pay money to have the sewage of the news, R-rated movies, pornography, and other things pumped into their homes.

If you're wondering why you are living in fear, things aren't going your way, or you just can't seem to stay positive, it's probably because you are saturating yourself with negativity!

Hope Deferred Makes the Heart Sick

Hope deferred maketh the heart sick: but when *the desire cometh,* it is *a tree of life.*

Proverbs 13:12

When things don't turn out the way you hoped for, you may experience disappointment. Even when your hope is simply deferred, the Scripture says it makes your heart sick. The body of Christ is the hope for this world. We can't afford to get discouraged. If we aren't encouraged and shining forth the light of God, I can guarantee, the ungodly aren't going to do it for us. So, we've got to keep ourselves encouraged.

A few years ago, Christian conservatives in the United States were hoping for a positive outcome from a presidential election. Instead, we learned that millions of Americans voted for candidates who supported ungodly policies. When things didn't go the way Christians hoped, many of them got discouraged.

We discovered that our nation was in a moral crisis. People were letting emotional issues influence them rather than the Word of God. Christians are the salt and light of the earth, but they have not been influencing the world enough to affect important events like elections. It is our responsibility to share the Gospel and give people hope. But many Christians give in to fear and discouragement if things don't turn out the way they think they should.

I haven't been depressed or discouraged for over fifty years. Now, I've had a lot of depressing things happen, and I've had a lot of opportunities to be depressed. But I've learned how to stand against it. The Lord really touched my life on March 23, 1968; and what happened to me then is more real to me now than it has ever been. Today, I am more encouraged, more full of faith, and have more vision for the future than I've ever had in my life.

What I'm saying is that this isn't just something that I'm just preaching in relation to what's going on in the news or anything like that. But for more than five decades, I have been able to maintain the intensity and joy of what's happened in my life. So, how do you keep your heart from getting sick?

Don't Let Your Heart Be Troubled

And ye shall hear of wars and rumours of wars: see that ye be not troubled: for all these things *must come to pass, but the end is not yet.*

Matthew 24:6

When it comes to being encouraged or discouraged, most people are up and down like a yo-yo. They have highs and lows, and they go into periods of just being depressed. But it doesn't have to be that way.

I have friends in Africa, and I've heard that there are groups like Boko Haram in Nigeria, who are murdering Christians right and left—taking young children and making them slaves. There are more Christians being martyred now for their faith than ever before in history.[1] We are living in a violent world. There are bad things going on and, sad to say, many Americans are fiddling while the world is burning. They just sit there and watch television and are basically desensitized to everything.

The truth is that there are *"wars and rumors of wars"* going on all around us, but Jesus said not to let your heart be troubled in the midst of these things. This is completely contrary to what most people think.

Most people think that if you are living in a bad situation, you can't help but be troubled. Unfortunately, today's church has been heavily influenced by psychology. If you stand up and say that you can bless the Lord at all times (Ps. 34:1) and praise God regardless of what's going on in your life, you will have a lot of Christians criticize you. They'll start saying you aren't compassionate, that you're making someone feel bad, or that you're condemning a person because they are struggling. I'm not condemning anyone, but I'm saying that you don't have to be depressed and discouraged. You can still rejoice and praise God no matter what outside circumstances look like.

I hope you understand this because it is really important. You can have control over your heart. You can determine whether or not you get depressed and discouraged. You can choose to bless the Lord instead. In John 16:33, Jesus said,

These things I have spoken unto you, that in me ye might have peace. In the world ye shall have tribulation: but be of good cheer; I have overcome the world.

This was the night before His crucifixion. Jesus knew he going to be arrested and then crucified. And yet, He told the disciples, "Don't let your heart be troubled" (John 14:1). He would be unjust to give someone that kind of a command if they couldn't do it.

Do What Is Right

For nation shall rise against nation, and kingdom against kingdom: and there shall be famines, and pestilences, and earthquakes, in divers places.

Matthew 24:7

We are experiencing famines today on an unprecedented scale.[2] Pestilences like the 2020 COVID pandemic dramatically affected the whole world. I've heard that even earthquakes are increasing at an exponential rate; there are more earthquakes happening today in different places than ever before.[3] Jesus talked about how these are signs of the end times.

In Matthew 24:8–9, Jesus says,

All these are *the beginning of sorrows. Then shall they deliver you up to be afflicted, and shall kill you: and ye shall be hated of all nations for my name's sake.*

I remember as a kid reading these verses and thinking, *Well, that applies for nations that don't know the Lord—not for America. In America, you'll never be hated for the cause of the Lord.* I'll tell you, things sure have changed.

It has become fashionable to criticize Christians. The Lord said you'd be *"hated of all nations"*—and that includes the United States. If you are standing for godly things, you will be criticized; you will be persecuted. While Christians in America are not currently facing the threat of dying for their faith, in a sense, criticism and shaming are more damaging forms of persecution. They are more subtle than open persecution and therefore more likely to weaken a person's resolve over time.

Right now, in America, no one is putting a gun to a Christian's head and saying, "You renounce your faith in the Lord, or I'll kill you!" But if taking a stand for Jesus is going to cost someone their job or acceptance among friends and family members, there are a lot of Christians who are not willing to pay that price. Sad to say, if many Christians were put on trial for their faith, there wouldn't be enough evidence to convict them. If you aren't being persecuted, it's because you aren't living godly (2 Tim. 3:12).

The time has come for Christians to stand up for what's right. And I can guarantee you will be persecuted. You will have people come out and call you a bigot, a homophobe, a hate monger, or something else, just because you say things like, "The Bible says that marriage is between a man and a woman." But that doesn't matter—you have to be bold and not afraid so that *"in the evil day … having done all, [you can] stand"* (Eph. 6:13).

Don't Be Corrupted

And turning the cities of Sodom and Gomorrha into ashes condemned them *with an overthrow, making* them *an ensample unto those that after should live ungodly.*

2 Peter 2:6

I've had people challenge me and say, "The Bible doesn't even mention homosexuality. That word's not even in the Bible!" The word *homosexual* wasn't even used until the 1800s,[4] so I will admit that the word is not in the Bible—but what happened to Sodom and Gomorrah (Gen. 19:1–25) is a pretty good indication of what God thinks of homosexuality.

The apostle Peter said God used Sodom and Gomorrah as an example to those who would follow after. He went on to say,

> *And delivered just Lot, vexed with the filthy conversation of the wicked: (for that righteous man dwelling among them, in seeing and hearing, vexed* his *righteous soul from day to day with* their *unlawful deeds;)*

> 2 Peter 2:7–8

Lot was a righteous, godly man. He loved God but he was *"vexed with the filthy conversation of the wicked … from day to day with their unlawful deeds."* Peter said that you vex your soul when you behold iniquity. This goes right along with Jesus saying,

> *because iniquity shall abound, the love of many shall wax cold.*

> Matthew 24:12

Not only will the evil things of the world get you into depression and discouragement, but they will also vex your soul.

There are still a lot of Christians who think, *Those things don't bother me. I can watch movies that have nudity, homosexuality, infidelity, lying, stealing, cursing, or profanity in them. I'm strong enough to be able to handle it.* I've had a lot of people tell me things like that. But the apostle Paul said in 1 Corinthians 15:33,

Be not deceived: evil communications corrupt good manners.

If you are a Christian and you say watching ungodly things doesn't bother you, then you're deceived. It will corrupt you. Your love for God and His people will wax (grow) cold. You'll become insensitive to the things of God, you'll be led by your feelings, and you won't stand on what the Bible says about these things.

Consider how candles were once made by hand. A person would take a wick and dip it in hot wax, pull it out and let it cool, then dip it in wax again to add another layer. After several times of doing this, the wax would build up until they had a candle. This is what happens to your heart when you are constantly exposed to iniquity. It waxes cold. It becomes hardened and insensitive through repeated exposure to ungodliness. That is a dangerous place to be as a believer!

Words Have Power

Death and life are *in the power of the tongue: and they that love it shall eat the fruit thereof.*

Proverbs 18:21

Words have life and death in them. When you listen to ungodliness, to lies, and to people who ridicule God and the Bible, you are exposing yourself to something deadly. Words are weapons. The Bible says,

No weapon that is formed against thee shall prosper; and every tongue that *shall rise against thee in judgment thou shalt condemn.*

Isaiah 54:17a

I'm not telling you to stick your head in the sand so you won't know what's going on in the world. But when you hear doubt, unbelief, and negativity, you have to condemn it. You have to stand against it. You have to say, "No, in the name of Jesus, this is not right!"

My wife Jamie will tell you that I'm fanatical about this. We'll be driving in the car and hear the news on the radio say, "It's flu season." And I'll respond, "Not for me, in the name of Jesus!" I'll talk back because words are weapons.

I believe I am redeemed from sickness and disease. And I don't believe I have to have those things. I've had sickness and disease in the past. But I am walking in divine health. I'm standing on the promises in God's Word— specifically those in Psalm 91.

Only with thine eyes shalt thou behold and see the reward of the wicked. Because thou hast made the Lord, which *is my refuge,* even *the most High, thy habitation; there shall no evil befall thee, neither shall any plague come nigh thy dwelling.*

Psalm 91:8–10

Many pastors have come against me saying, "Andrew Wommack doesn't believe he can get sick." Now, I'll admit, I'm capable of getting sick, just the same as anybody else. But I've been appropriating God's healing promises and walking in them. And it has been decades since I have had any sickness.

If you hear unbelief, counter it, and speak against it. As you do this, negativity will lose its impact. But you have to condemn and counter these things because every word you hear in music, news, movies, and other places brings either life or death. This even applies to the words of your own mouth! If you don't resist and say, "No, in the name of Jesus," then those words are like seeds that immediately start producing death.

Get in the Word

And David was greatly distressed; for the people spake of stoning him, because the soul of all the people was grieved, every man for his sons and for his daughters: but David encouraged himself in the Lord his God.

1 Samuel 30:6

I encourage myself and stay positive by reading and meditating on the Bible. The Word of God has to become dominant in your life. If your love is waxing cold because of things that are happening around you, it's because you are more plugged in to the world than you are to the Word of God.

You could study nearly every noteworthy person in the Bible and learn things from their lives. Every one of them experienced adversity—things that would have discouraged them and even destroyed them. Scripture shows us how to overcome these things.

Now all these things happened unto them for ensamples: and they are written for our admonition, upon whom the ends of the world are come.

1 Corinthians 10:11

Everything in the Old Testament was recorded for our benefit, so that we might learn not to be discouraged and learn how to overcome certain things. If you are facing anything difficult or negative right now, I promise you that someone in the Bible has faced things as bad or worse than what you are going through. And the Scripture shows you how they overcame it. This is how you encourage yourself in the Lord and keep from becoming negative when everything around you seems to be going wrong.

We can look at what David went through because he was anointed to be king at seventeen years old (2 Sam. 5:3–4) while Saul was still on the throne. For the next thirteen years, it seemed like everything went wrong for David.

David had to flee for his life from his father-in-law, King Saul. Saul took David's wife, Michal, and gave her to another man just to hurt David. Then Saul tried multiple times to kill David. All this time, David refused to kill Saul, even though he would been justified in the eyes of the people for all the things the king had done to him.

There were six hundred men who followed David, and while he and his army were with the Philistines, they left the town of Ziklag unprotected. That was where their families were staying. Seeing an opening, the Amalekites attacked Ziklag, burned the town, took all their possessions, all their wives, and all their children. It's a long story, but it looked like David and his men had lost everything. It would have been easy for David to get depressed and discouraged, and throw up his hands and say, "What's the use? Why keep fighting?"

Encourage Yourself in the Lord

But ye, beloved, building up yourselves on your most holy faith, praying in the Holy Ghost, keep yourselves in the love of God, looking for the mercy of our Lord Jesus Christ unto eternal life.

Jude 20–21

For thirteen years, David had been persecuted. He had to run for his life, people betrayed him, and he even had to act like he was crazy in front of the Philistines (1 Sam. 21:13). David had been through terrible things already, and the men who had been with him wanted to stone him.

David had done many good things for them, but because they had seen their city burned and their wives and children taken captive, they were going to kill him. This would have been a great opportunity to quit and just give up. David was in a very negative situation. But look at the last phrase in 1 Samuel 30:6:

David encouraged himself in the Lord his God.

That's powerful.

Most people don't know how to encourage themselves in the Lord. They depend upon others, such as a minister or other Christians. Now, people can play a role in that encouragement through fellowship. The Bible says we are supposed to encourage one another:

Take heed, brethren, lest there be in any of you an evil heart of unbelief, in departing from the living God. But exhort one another daily, while it is called To day; lest any of you be hardened through the deceitfulness of sin.

Hebrews 3:12–13

Relationships are an important a part of the Christian life, but you shouldn't always depend on another person. You can't always run to someone else to have them pray for you. You need to learn how to encourage yourself in the Lord.

I thank God that I've learned how to encourage myself in the Lord. This is what is missing in so many people's lives. They are dependent upon other people, but nobody can be there for you the way the Lord will be.

The Holy Spirit was specifically given to born-again believers to build them up. The Holy Spirit is called the Comforter (John 14:16–17). So, if you have the baptism of the Holy Spirit, I have compassion for you; but I don't have sympathy for you if you're discouraged or depressed. You've got the greatest gift God ever gave us. You can build yourself up praying in tongues (Jude 20). It's just like flipping a switch and turning on the power of the Holy Spirit. If you're discouraged, it's because you aren't using what you've got. You've got to learn how to encourage yourself.

Seek God's Wisdom

And David said to Abiathar the priest, Ahimelech's son, I pray thee, bring me hither the ephod. And Abiathar brought thither the ephod to David. And David enquired at the Lord, saying, Shall I pursue after this troop? shall I overtake them? And he answered him, Pursue: for thou shalt surely overtake them, *and without fail recover* all.

1 Samuel 30:7–8

David encouraged himself in the Lord by seeking wisdom and direction from Him. The ephod was a garment that the priest wore, and it was used to inquire of the Lord.

David asked, "Should I pursue the Amalekites and overtake them?" And the Lord said, "Yes, you will overtake them and recover everything, so pursue them."

In this battle, they took back all their wives and children, along with all their possessions and all the spoil of the Amalekites. They actually ended up with more than they had before and, within a couple of days, David became the king of Israel. What he had been believing for thirteen years came to pass in a matter of hours. This happened right after it seemed all was lost.

When you are fighting the negativity of all that is happening around you, how do you encourage yourself in the Lord? You turn to God's Word. When you reach a place where it seems like you can't stand it anymore and have reached your limit, stand on 1 Corinthians 10:13:

There hath no temptation taken you but such as is common to man: but God is *faithful, who will not suffer you to be tempted above that ye are able; but will with the temptation also make a way to escape, that ye may be able to bear* it*.*

God won't let you go beyond your limit. When you reach a place where, like David, you've wept until you can't weep anymore (1 Sam. 30:4), that means that if you just keep standing, God is going to come through for you. David was right at the breaking point, and it was only a matter of hours until his vision and his dreams came to pass. It can be the same for you.

Renew Your Mind

The law of the Lord is *perfect, converting the soul: the testimony of the Lord* is *sure, making wise the simple.*

Psalm 19:7

I keep myself encouraged by turning to the Word of God. With all the negative things going on in the world right now, this is so important. But the average Christian does not spend much time in the Bible. They spend more time in the light of their television than they do in the light of God's Word.

If you spend more time listening to what the world says than what the Word of God says, you aren't going to be encouraged. You will be discouraged. Your love will grow cold (Matt. 24:12). Some people say, "Well, I don't have a lot of quantity time in God's Word, but I have quality time." That just won't work. You've got to spend more time in the Word than you do in the world.

You can't just be plugged in to television and the internet. If you let the sewage of the world flow through your mind, some of it's going to stick on the inside of you, and you'll get clogged up. You're deceived if you think media, news, and television are not going to affect you.

During the 2020 COVID pandemic, when the rest of the world was glued to the news and panicking, I spent five to ten hours a day in the Bible. I love the Word of God and get great things out of it. Psalm 119:97 says,

O how love I thy law! it is *my meditation all the day.*

I love the Word of God more than I love movies, television shows, sports, or anything else. It speaks to me. I can barely open the Bible without God just shouting at me. It changes my perception. I begin to see things through the light of what God's Word says rather than what the world says. If you are going to encourage yourself in the Lord, as David did (1 Sam. 30:6), you have to seek direction from God's Word. It's the foundation of everything.

When you are born again, your spirit is made new and perfect (2 Cor. 5:17). But your mind (which is part of your soul) needs to be renewed by the Word of God (Rom. 12:2). You do this by planting the seed of God's Word in your heart. The Word of God is perfect, and it will restore your soul to the condition that God wants it to be. If your soul is not where it's supposed to be, you need to spend more time in God's Word.

Let Your Heart Rejoice

The statutes of the Lord are *right, rejoicing the heart: the commandment of the Lord* is *pure, enlightening the eyes.*

Psalm 19:8

If you're in the Word of God, it will cause you to rejoice. It will give you joy and peace. If your heart's not rejoicing, you need to be in the Word of God.

When I was in the Army at Fort Hamilton, New York, I witnessed to every person I could find, and they hated me because of it. They treated me like the plague. I was in a barracks with about fifty people, and for six weeks not a single person talked to me. When I'd go sit down next to somebody, they'd pick up their stuff and move. It began to bother me, and I was feeling sorry for myself. My heart wasn't rejoicing.

One Saturday, while everybody else went into New York City, I stayed in the barracks. I was the only person there, and I spent my time studying the Word for eight hours. I just sat on my bunk and read the Bible. And after eight hours of being in the Word, I could have run through a troop or leaped over a wall (Ps. 18:29). The contrast between the joy that I experienced after being in the Word and the discouragement and the rejection I felt from others was like night and day.

If you're discouraged, it's because you aren't in the Word of God, you're not encouraging yourself in the Lord, and you're not building yourself up by praying in tongues. You're discouraged and depressed because you're letting circumstances dominate you. You are looking at things in the natural. Put your eyes on the Word of God, and if you do that, it'll rejoice your heart.

When you get into the Bible, it will also help you see things differently. It will enlighten your eyes. People who aren't in the Word of God are like people who are walking in the dark. You just can't see everything, and it's just a matter of time till you bump into something. But when you're in the Word of God, it enlightens your eyes. It enables you to see things, you'll magnify God, and you will see Him as bigger than whatever problem you're facing.

Keep Your Heart Clean

The fear of the Lord is *clean, enduring for ever: the judgments of the Lord* are *true and righteous altogether.*

Psalm 19:9

There aren't a lot of things in this world that are clean. There just seems to be impurity in everything. Even if you find a movie that you like, there's going to be some sort of junk in it.

I once heard a story about a pastor whose son wanted to go to the movies with his friends. The boy asked his dad if he could go. The pastor asked, "What's the movie rated?" So, the boy told him, and the pastor said, "No, that's not the kind of movie I want you to see." His son argued, "Well, everybody else is going! The deacons' kids are going! There's just a tiny bit of nudity; there are just a few curse words in it. Overall, it's a good movie." But the pastor still said, "No."

Then, that pastor used some wisdom. He told his son that, instead of going to watch the movie, he could invite some of his friends over to the house. When the kids were all playing in the backyard, the pastor brought some brownies out to them for a snack. They were hot out of the oven and probably looked delicious. But as this pastor gave the brownies to the kids, he said, "Before you eat these, I just want you to know that there's a little bit of dog poop in them. There's not much. You won't taste it, it won't make you sick, and it shouldn't bother you at all, but I just want you to know there's a little bit of dog poop in there." Of course, none of those kids wanted to eat the brownies, but the pastor had made his point.

This is the way a lot of Christians are. They think, *Well, there's only a little bit of nudity, hatred, and strife in it, but overall, it seems good.* By contrast, the Word of God is pure. It's clean. It endures forever. *"The judgments of the Lord are true and righteous altogether"* (Ps. 19:9b). Again, there's very little in our world today that's true and righteous altogether. You need to stay in the Word of God if you want to keep your heart clean and stay encouraged.

Don't Believe a Negative Report

And there we saw the giants, the sons of Anak, which come of the giants: and we were in our own sight as grasshoppers, and so we were in their sight.
Numbers 13:33

To me this is the most amazing example of negativism. Moses sent spies to evaluate the Promised Land. He didn't send them to find out if they *could* take the land. They were just supposed to report where the strongholds were.

Several years ago, I was in Washington, DC, with my friend David Barton of WallBuilders. He occasionally leads tours of the Capitol and Statuary Hall and shares how many of our founders were clergymen who loved God. It's powerful! While we were there, members of Congress spoke to us, and they were all godly people. I learned they meet together and pray every day.

After two days of seeing the Capitol and hearing these congressional leaders come in and speak, I admitted to David that I had no idea things were so good in this nation. Everything I had been hearing in the news was about how terrible everything is. David responded by saying, "You've been listening to the 'ten spies' network."

This is what happened to the Israelites, a group of about three million people. When Moses sent the twelve spies out, they came back and said,

> *We came unto the land whither thou sentest us, and surely it floweth with milk and honey; and this* is *the fruit of it.*

Numbers 13:27

They brought back one cluster of grapes on a pole in between two men because it was so large (Num. 13:23). Those grapes must have been as big as apples! But then they said,

> *Nevertheless the people* be *strong that dwell in the land, and the cities* are *walled,* and *very great: and moreover we saw the children of Anak there.*
>
> Numbers 13:28

Ten spies discouraged the Israelites by saying,

> *We be not able to go up against the people; for they are stronger than we … And there we saw the giants, the sons of Anak, which come of the giants: and we were in our own sight as grasshoppers, and so we were in their sight.*
>
> Numbers 13:31,33

Only two spies—Joshua and Caleb—urged the Israelites to enter the land without fear because the Lord was with them. (Num. 13:30, 14:6-9) Unfortunately, the Israelites did not listen to Joshua and Caleb.

Everything the spies said was true. But you've got to take the truth and put it into the proper perspective. More than forty years later, when Joshua sent two spies to Jericho they came to Rahab's house. She told them the people had heard how God parted the Red Sea (Ex. 14:21–29) and how the kings of the Amorites were destroyed (Num. 21:21–35).

> *And as soon as we had heard* these things, *our hearts did melt, neither did there remain any more courage in any man, because of you: for the Lord your God, he* is *God in heaven above, and in earth beneath.*
>
> Joshua 2:11

If the Israelites had known what the people in the Promised Land were actually feeling—if they would have believed Joshua and Caleb instead of the other ten spies—they could have just walked right in and taken the land. They would have had no problem. Instead, they were discouraged by a negative report, and everyone twenty years old and older died in the wilderness because of it (Num. 14:29).

You Don't Need All the Details

> *But thanks* be *to God, which giveth us the victory through our Lord Jesus Christ.*
>
> 1 Corinthians 15:57

The Lord wants us to live by faith. He doesn't just show a person the end from the beginning. If people knew the end from the beginning and what they'd have to deal with to get there, many of them would be impatient and wouldn't take time to grow. They would try to make things come to pass on their own. On the other hand, some people would be so overwhelmed with what God showed them that they would run the other direction. But the things of God come step by step.

Over the years I have recognized a pattern: every twelve years something miraculous happens in my life and ministry. On the morning of August 26, 2019—at the end one of these twelve-year segments—I was praising and worshiping God for all the good things He had done. I asked God, "What's going to happen in the next twelve years?" Immediately, I got the response, "You don't want to know!" Even though I *did* want to know, there was silence after that. God had given me an answer, and He wasn't going to argue with me about it.

That was right before the COVID pandemic of 2020, and all the lockdowns and mandates associated with it. The government declared that churches were nonessential and tried to stop people from worshipping together. We even received a cease-and-desist letter during one of our events here at Charis. I could have been arrested. The State of Colorado sued us, and we sued them.

Eventually, the U.S. Supreme Court ruled in favor of some churches in other states that fought back against lockdowns. Because of that, Colorado backed down, and we came through it. Now, the Holy Spirit did show my staff some strategies that helped us continue ministering through that time, but I'm glad I didn't know exactly what was going to happen. I was walking by faith, and I trusted Him. I just knew we were going to win if we didn't quit.

God doesn't show you everything. He didn't show the Israelites that when they got to Jericho, the walls would fall down, and they would win automatically. He just promised them that they would possess the land—that it was already a done deal. The Lord promises victory, but He doesn't give you all the details. You must walk by faith and trust Him. You have to be encouraged by His promises.

Personalize God's Promises

For all the promises of God in him are *yea, and in him Amen, unto the glory of God by us.*

2 Corinthians 1:20

All of us have general promises from the Lord, but many people haven't personalized the Word of God. You may read this scripture and think, *Well, God promised this to Paul, not me.* But for God's promises to work in your life, they must become personal to you.

This is why so many people are going through life without direction. You may be doing your own thing and asking God to bless it. You may be praying, "God, bless my business," or "God, bless my decision." But I don't ever ask God to bless what I'm doing. I don't do things that are of my own choosing. Instead, I seek the Lord, and I wait until God tells me to do something.

If God tells you to do something, it's already blessed. To try and get God to bless your plan is wrong. You need to raise a white flag, surrender by becoming a living sacrifice, and then renew your mind to what God tells you to do (Rom. 12:1–2). When you do that, you're automatically blessed. But that only begins when you begin personalizing the Word of God.

I had an experience with the Lord that helped me understand this. The Lord woke me up in the middle of the night not long after Jamie and I were married. The presence of God was so real I just sat there for hours, afraid to open my eyes. Finally, the Lord asked me, "What do you want?"

God told me He was giving me the same choice that He gave Solomon (1 Kgs. 3:5); I could pick anything I wanted from Him. At that time, I was an introvert. I'd been trying to minister the Word for a couple of years by then, and it was just pitiful. I was afraid of people and froze every time I got up in front of a group.

After one of my meetings, someone came up to me and said, "You've got some really good things to share. If you would love the people more than you loved yourself, you could be a blessing." What this man said felt like getting stabbed by a knife, but he was right. I was worried about what other people thought about me. Things needed to change.

In response to God's offer, I said, "I want the ability to speak your Word without fear." So, the Lord touched me and put His words in my mouth, just like He promised the prophet Jeremiah.

Then the word of the Lord came unto me, saying, Before I formed thee in the belly I knew thee; and before thou camest forth out of the womb I sanctified thee, and *I ordained thee a prophet unto the nations. Then said I, Ah, Lord God! behold, I cannot speak: for I* am *a child. But the Lord said unto me, Say not, I* am *a child: for thou shalt go to all that I shall send thee, and whatsoever I command thee thou shalt speak. Be not afraid of their faces: for I* am *with thee to deliver thee, saith the Lord. Then the Lord put forth his hand, and touched my mouth. And the Lord said unto me, Behold, I have put my words in thy mouth.*

Jeremiah 1:4-9

Those scriptures became mine. God may have spoken them to Jeremiah, but through His Word, the Lord also spoke that to me. I personalized God's Word, and it totally transformed my life. Now I speak to potentially billions of people every day through our *Gospel Truth* television program.

God has given promises to me and to you. You just need to believe them and make them your own.

Use Your Imagination

Verily, verily, I say unto you, He that believeth on me, the works that I do shall he do also; and greater works *than these shall he do; because I go unto my Father.*

John 14:12

Once you personalize God's promises and believe them, then you need to visualize them coming to pass. If you have trouble believing what the Lord says about you, you just need to change your perspective. You can change your life by changing what you see in your heart—your imagination.

Many people can quote the healing promises of God, e.g., *"by whose stripes ye were healed"* (1 Pet. 2:24); *"Himself took our infirmities, and bare* our *sicknesses"* (Matt. 8:17); and *"He sent his word, and healed them"* (Ps. 107:20). But many of those same people still see themselves sick in their imaginations. If you can't see yourself healed on the inside, you'll never see it on the outside. You must take the Word of God, make it personal to you, and then visualize those promises in your own life.

I took John 14:12 and made that scripture my own. Jesus spoke that to me. I personalized it and said, "Father, you told me that, and yet I haven't seen those things come to pass." So, I just focused on doing the works that Jesus did and didn't even worry about the greater works. Then, I started saying, "Father, I want to see the dead raised!"

I looked up every scripture in the Bible where a person was raised from the dead, wrote them out on a piece of paper, and I started meditating on them. That allowed the Word to come alive on the inside of me. As I started meditating and thinking on these scriptures, I saw Jesus raising Lazarus from the dead in my imagination (John 11:38–44). Then, I meditated on it until I saw myself raising Lazarus from the dead.

I got to the point where I would dream every night of raising twenty to thirty people from the dead. After a while, it just consumed me. Not long after seeing these things in my imagination, they moved from the spiritual into the natural. A man died in one of my meetings, and we saw him raised from the dead.

That was awesome! But ten to fifteen years went by, and I thought, *I haven't seen anybody raised from the dead lately*. So, I went back and started meditating on these scriptures and began dreaming about it and seeing it on the inside of me again. Soon after that, my son died and was dead for five hours. But Jamie and I believed God, and he came back from the dead. Praise the Lord!

What Picture Is Inside You?

As you consistently meditate on the Word, you'll eventually reach a point that you won't know how to *disbelieve* God. You don't have to be plagued with doubt. Sad to say, most Christians don't understand this. They think that it's normal to constantly live with doubt, always wondering what God is going to do. You won't be able to stay positive in negative circumstances if you think that way.

Once, my board of directors sent me to the doctor for a stress test because of an insurance policy application. As the doctor began prepping me for the treadmill, his nurse asked if they could shave the hair off my chest to give the electrodes a place to stick. "You can't shave my chest," I said. "This is virgin hair. It's never been touched!" They tried to stick those things to my chest without shaving it, but about thirteen minutes into the test, they started falling off. To finish, I had to hold two electrodes in place, the nurse held two, and the doctor held two more.

When I finished, the doctor looked over my results. Then he started grunting and writing on my chart. When he finally looked up at me, he said, "Here's the name of a doctor I know. He's a specialist. I want you to go over there and get tested right away. We may admit you into the hospital for open-heart surgery before the day is over."

I was shocked! I didn't feel ill. I began thinking about the image of health and strength God's Word had on the inside of me, and I said to him, "That's a lie. I don't believe it. You look at that readout again and tell me that it says I have a heart problem."

The doctor just looked at me (probably because he wasn't used to people calling him a liar) and said, "Well, it doesn't really say you have a heart problem. It just says that there was an abnormality during testing. It may be nothing, but it could be something serious. We need to get you tested." He didn't consider the fact that those electrodes were falling off my chest!

"That's not what you told me," I said, getting mad. "You told me I might have to have open-heart surgery before the day is over. You lied to me!"

The doctor tore up the test results and said, "Fine! You're on your own! Get out of here!"

Later, I had a nuclear stress test done, which was more accurate than a treadmill test; and I was told that I had the heart of a seventeen-year-old. I had been meditating on

God's promises about healing so when the first doctor told me I needed open-heart surgery, I didn't believe him. And, praise God, I didn't need surgery. I kept a positive attitude because I focused on God's Word.

Don't Let Yourself Be Tempted

Be not deceived; God is not mocked: for whatsoever a man soweth, that shall he also reap.

Galatians 6:7

Back to the story of when I witnessed to people in New York City… I remember going to 42nd Street. There must have been a hundred prostitutes lined up along a wall, but I wasn't sharp enough to realize what they were doing. I just thought, *This is awesome! Here are all these women I can witness to!* So, I went down the row, gave each of them a tract, started preaching, and I cleaned out the entire street. They all left!

At some point, a pimp came up to me and tried to sell me one of his girls. He was using all this street language, but I just couldn't understand him. Because I was so naive, it just didn't register. After a few minutes, this pimp just threw up his hands, shook his head, and walked off! He must have been thinking, *What rock did this guy crawl out from under?*

When I got back to the hotel room, I started explaining what happened to the guys I was staying with. I said, "You will never believe what this guy was saying to me!" And I started telling them what that pimp said. They started laughing and told me he was trying to sell one of his prostitutes. Thank God I didn't know what he had been talking about. Because I loved God and wanted to serve Him, I ended up witnessing to everyone on the street about Jesus.

Through that whole experience, I didn't know enough to be tempted because I had never thought about it. It didn't dawn on me that people would do things like that. I didn't have to pray, "Oh Jesus, help me to resist!" I didn't have to resist anything. I just had a positive outlook.

You can't be tempted with what you don't think about (Heb. 11:15). The reason some of you are tempted to commit adultery is because you watch movies and television shows that portray adultery. It affects you emotionally, and you end up drawn to it.

A person doesn't just wake up one day and commit adultery. Before a person sins, they conceive it in their imagination. When you watch things that show someone being unfaithful in marriage, it plants a seed in your heart. And what you put in your heart, good or bad, will bear fruit. If you sow God's Word into your heart, you'll see God's best begin to manifest in your life. If you sow the things of this world, it will bear sin.

If you're struggling with temptations, it's because you're thinking about negative reports or ungodly things in the world. You can't be tempted with something you don't think about. So, quit thinking about it, and you won't be tempted!

Draw on Your Relationship with God

But he refused, and said unto his master's wife, Behold, my master wotteth not what is *with me in the house, and he hath committed all that he hath to my hand;* there is *none greater in this house than I; neither hath he kept back any thing from me but thee, because thou* art *his wife: how then can I do this great wickedness, and sin against God?*

Genesis 39:8–9

When I was serving in the Army in Vietnam, the U.S. military would occasionally bring the troops out of the field and back to headquarters in Chu Lai (on the South China Sea) for what they called a "standdown." For three days, they would give troops all the alcohol they could drink. They also brought in women and put on a musical show that was sexually oriented. It turned out these women were prostitutes, so a person could have all the booze, drugs, and sex they wanted for three days—all funded by the U.S. government.

I was in a company of two hundred people, and every time they'd bring us back for stand down, I was the only person who did not go to the shows and participate. I could hear all the music and yelling going on in that pavilion, but I would just sit on the beach while all that debauchery went on around me.

All that noise was like a magnet drawing me because I wanted to be accepted. I'll admit, I didn't enjoy being treated like the plague by the other soldiers back at Fort Hamilton. (If you like being persecuted, there's something wrong with you!) But God was speaking to me through Joseph's words, *"How then can I do this great wickedness, and sin against God?"* Because I had spent all that time in the Bible, I was able to personalize God's Word, and He spoke to me through it.

Joseph resisted the temptation of Potiphar's wife and, even though he suffered because of his choice, he stayed positive. Everything in his life seemed headed in a negative direction for thirteen years, but one day he ended up going from the pit to the palace because he stood on God's promises, saw them come to pass in his imagination, and stayed positive.

There was another guy in Vietnam who had grown up the same church I did, and we had known each other our entire lives. We weren't staying in the exact same location in Vietnam, but we saw each other often. Even though he had the same upbringing as I did, this guy wound up giving in to temptation because he wasn't encouraging himself in the Lord.

Choose Your Mold

And be not conformed to this world: but be ye transformed by the renewing of your mind, that ye may prove what is *that good, and acceptable, and perfect, will of God.*

Romans 12:2

Satan will try to put you in a position to compromise. But if you have a relationship with God, His Word will keep you from becoming depressed, discouraged, and an easy target for the enemy's attacks. It is so important to stay positive, to personalize God's promises, and to see yourself receiving God's best.

Even though I felt drawn to be a part of what other people were doing in Vietnam and to be accepted by them, I loved God more than I loved people. I had learned not to rely on other people to encourage me. I relied upon my relationship with the Lord to help me stay positive in a negative situation.

This is just my personal opinion, but I think post-traumatic stress disorder isn't just from the torments of war. The typical soldier indulges in sinful behavior with prostitutes, drugs, and alcohol. They do things in war that they would never do back home, where they would be accountable to a spouse or a family, father or mother, sister or brother, or anyone else.

Their guilt and shame are eating them up on the inside. So, when they come home, they may struggle with what they saw during battle, but I think that there's also guilt over other things that happened.

Remember, because I loved God and was focused on serving Him, I didn't even recognize prostitution when it was right in front of me—even when it was offered to me! I'm not saying these things to brag, but it was because I was encouraging myself in God. I had a positive outlook, even when I was surrounded by evil, ungodly, and negative things.

Having been drafted in the military during wartime meant the possibility of being killed in action. So, when we received our orders to be deployed to Vietnam, a bunch of the men started crying because they knew what that meant.

There was a chaplain there who shared something that really blessed me. He told us that the Army was like a fire, and it would melt you. "But," he said, "you get to choose what mold you're poured into." As it turned out, what could have been a very negative experience ended up being one of the best things that ever happened to me. By the time I got back from Vietnam, I had been spending up to fifteen hours a day studying the Bible—and I was stronger than horseradish!

Conclusion

While people around me were letting their experience in Vietnam conform them to this world and get into ungodly behaviors, I chose a different mold. I let the Word of God transform me. I chose to stay positive, and the Lord set me on a course that led me to where we are today!

Through Charis Bible College and the *Gospel Truth* television program, we are changing lives all around the world. We've had opportunities over the years to be discouraged and depressed when we were struggling financially, and it seemed like people were staying away from our meetings by the thousands. But we didn't quit! Now, it's all we can do just to keep up with everything the Lord is doing!

Again, God is no respecter of persons. What the Lord did for me, I believe He can do for you. But you have a part to play. The will of God doesn't come to pass automatically. You have to plant the seed of God's Word (1 Pet. 1:23) in your heart if you want it to bear fruit (Gal. 5:22–23).

If you just passively let the things of this world affect your life, you'll let fear overtake you, and you will be discouraged. It's time for the body of Christ to take a stand against ungodliness. But it's going to take believers standing on the Word of God, personalizing His promises, and using their imagination to see the Lord's will come to pass and be a force for good!

I believe if we stay positive in a negative world, we will see things change! With God, all things are possible, and the best is yet to come!

FURTHER STUDY

If you enjoyed this booklet and would like to learn more about some of the things I've shared, I suggest my teachings:

- *Christian First-Aid Kit*
- *Harnessing Your Emotions*
- *The True Nature of God*
- *The Effects of Praise*
- *10 Reasons It's Better to Have the Holy Spirit*

These teachings are available for free at **awmi.net**, or they can be purchased at **awmi.net/store**.

Receive Jesus as Your Savior

Choosing to receive Jesus Christ as your Lord and Savior is the most important decision you'll ever make!

God's Word promises, *"That if thou shalt confess with thy mouth the Lord Jesus, and shalt believe in thine heart that God hath raised him from the dead, thou shalt be saved. For with the heart man believeth unto righteousness; and with the mouth confession is made unto salvation"* (Rom. 10:9–10). *"For whosoever shall call upon the name of the Lord shall be saved"* (Rom. 10:13). By His grace, God has already done everything to provide salvation. Your part is simply to believe and receive.

Pray out loud: "Jesus, I acknowledge that I've sinned and need to receive what you did for the forgiveness of my sins. I confess that You are my Lord and Savior. I believe in my heart that God raised You from the dead. By faith in Your Word, I receive salvation now. Thank You for saving me."

The very moment you commit your life to Jesus Christ, the truth of His Word instantly comes to pass in your spirit. Now that you're born again, there's a brand-new you!

Please contact us and let us know that you've prayed to receive Jesus as your Savior. We'd like to send you some free materials to help you on your new journey. Call our Helpline: **719-635-1111** (available 24 hours a day, seven days a week) to speak to a staff member who is here to help you understand and grow in your new relationship with the Lord.

Welcome to your new life!

Receive the Holy Spirit

As His child, your loving heavenly Father wants to give you the supernatural power you need to live a new life. *"For every one that asketh receiveth; and he that seeketh findeth; and to him that knocketh it shall be opened…how much more shall* your *heavenly Father give the Holy Spirit to them that ask him?"* (Luke 11:10–13).

All you have to do is ask, believe, and receive! Pray this: "Father, I recognize my need for Your power to live a new life. Please fill me with Your Holy Spirit. By faith, I receive it right now. Thank You for baptizing me. Holy Spirit, You are welcome in my life."

Some syllables from a language you don't recognize will rise up from your heart to your mouth (1 Cor. 14:14). As you speak them out loud by faith, you're releasing God's power from within and building yourself up in the spirit (1 Cor. 14:4). You can do this whenever and wherever you like.

It doesn't really matter whether you felt anything or not when you prayed to receive the Lord and His Spirit. If you believed in your heart that you received, then God's Word promises you did. *"Therefore I say unto you, What things soever ye desire, when ye pray, believe that ye receive* them*, and ye shall have* them*"* (Mark 11:24). God always honors His Word—believe it!

We would like to rejoice with you, pray with you, and answer any questions to help you understand more fully what has taken place in your life!

Please contact us to let us know that you've prayed to be filled with the Holy Spirit and to request the book *The New You & the Holy Spirit*. This book will explain in more detail about the benefits of being filled with the Holy Spirit and speaking in tongues. Call our Helpline: **719-635-1111** (available 24 hours a day, seven days a week).

Endnotes

1. Cristina Maza, "Christian Persecution and Genocide Is Worse Now Than 'Any Time in History,' Report Says," *Newsweek*, January 4, 2018, https://www.newsweek.com/christian-persecution-genocide-worse-ever-770462.

2. "A Global Food Crisis," World Food Programme, accessed October 2, 2023, https://www.wfp.org/global-hunger-crisis.

3. Jessica Onsurez, "Is New Mexico Ready for Increasing Earthquakes?" *Carlsbad Current-Argus*, July 6, 2023, https://www.currentargus.com/story/opinion/editorials/2023/07/06/reporting-tackles-increased-number-of-earthquakes-shaking-new-mexico/70196818007/; "UH Research Investigates Increase in Pāhala Earthquakes," *University of Hawaii News*, June 30, 2022, https://www.hawaii.edu/news/2022/06/30/uh-research-increase-in-pahala-earthquakes/.

4. *Merriam-Webster Dictionary*, s.v. "homosexual." Accessed October 2, 2023, https://www.merriam-webster.com/dictionary/homosexual.

Call for Prayer

If you need prayer for any reason, you can call our Helpline, 24 hours a day, seven days a week at **719-635-1111**. A trained prayer minister will answer your call and pray with you.

Every day, we receive testimonies of healings and other miracles from our Helpline, and we are ministering God's nearly-too-good-to-be-true message of the Gospel to more people than ever. So, I encourage you to call today!

About the Author

Andrew Wommack's life was forever changed the moment he encountered the supernatural love of God on March 23, 1968. As a renowned Bible teacher and author, Andrew has made it his mission to change the way the world sees God.

Andrew's vision is to go as far and deep with the Gospel as possible. His message goes far through the *Gospel Truth* television program, which is available to over half the world's population. The message goes deep through discipleship at Charis Bible College, headquartered in Woodland Park, Colorado. Founded in 1994, Charis has campuses across the United States and around the globe.

Andrew also has an extensive library of teaching materials in print, audio, and video. More than 200,000 hours of free teachings can be accessed at **awmi.net**.

Contact Information

Andrew Wommack Ministries, Inc.

PO Box 3333
Colorado Springs, CO 80934-3333
info@awmi.net
awmi.net

Helpline: 719-635-1111 (available 24/7)

Charis Bible College

info@charisbiblecollege.org
844-360-9577
CharisBibleCollege.org

For a complete list of all of our offices,
visit **awmi.net/contact-us**.

Connect with us on social media.

There's more on the website!

Discover FREE teachings, testimonies, and more by scanning the QR code.

Continue to grow in the Word of God! You'll be blessed!

ANDREW WOMMACK MINISTRIES

Your monthly giving makes the greatest kingdom impact.

When you give, you make an impact in the kingdom that lasts for generations. Your generosity enables our phone ministers to answer calls 24/7. Your support is also expanding Charis Bible College and allowing *The Gospel Truth* to reach an even wider global audience. You do this and more through your giving each month!

Become a Grace Partner today!

Andrew's LIVING COMMENTARY BIBLE SOFTWARE

Andrew Wommack's *Living Commentary* Bible study software is a user-friendly, downloadable program. It's like reading the Bible with Andrew at your side, sharing his revelation with you verse by verse.

Main features:
- Bible study software with a grace-and-faith perspective
- Over 26,000 notes by Andrew on verses from Genesis through Revelation
- *Matthew Henry's Concise Commentary*
- 12 Bible versions
- 2 concordances: *Englishman's Concordance* and *Strong's Concordance*
- 2 dictionaries: *Collaborative International Dictionary* and *Holman's Dictionary*
- Atlas with biblical maps
- Bible and *Living Commentary* statistics
- Quick navigation, including history of verses
- Robust search capabilities (for the Bible and Andrew's notes)
- "Living" (i.e., constantly updated and expanding)
- Ability to create personal notes

Whether you're new to studying the Bible or a seasoned Bible scholar, you'll gain a deeper revelation of the Word from a grace-and-faith perspective.

Purchase Andrew's *Living Commentary* today at **awmi.net/living**, and grow in the Word with Andrew.

ANDREW WOMMACK MINISTRIES

Item code: 8350